Excerpts by Iakovos Kambanellis from **"Freedom Came in May"**, 2nd edition.

© EPHELANT Publishing, Dr Richard Reiter, Vienna 2018. Copyright reserved. ISBN: 978-3-900766-27-6

Translated from German by Patricia Hughes
© Patricia Hughes 3.9.2019 Hues Books
ISBN 9781909275348

With the support of the Austrian Republic's National Fund for Victims of National Socialism Funds for the Future, Advancement of Science and Research in the Austrian Republic, State of Upper Austria, and city of Vienna.

CHRISTIAN ANGERER

GOOD SIGNS

Freedom Came in May

Translated from German by
Patricia Hughes

	Introduction and Biography	7
1.	A state with deadly borders	14
	The concentration camp and its surroundings	15
	Everybody knew	19
2	The SS in the concentration camp	20
	The football field	21
3	Admitting prisoners into the camp	23
	Photo: Inmate beside the Wailing Wall	25
4	Rulers and forced labour in the concentration camp	26
	Poem 'Andonis'	30
5	Solidarity in the concentration camp	33
	Strength to carry on	35
6	Life after liberation	37
	Poem: When the war is over	
7	Concentration camp and community	41
	No State within a State	45

Introduction and Biography

Iakovos Kambanellis wrote 'Freedom came in May' as a result of time spent in Mauthausen Concentration camp in Upper Austria; the title refers to his unexpected release by American forces in May 1945. His personal memoir is of being arrested with no recourse in law, and of freight journeys between different camps. At the same time ordinary people completely ignored those heading for the camps as they went about their normal lives. It was proof of Hannah Arendt's "banality of evil". Further proof is given in the lack of human language for detainees. Human beings controlled as units or numbers are remade as non-human, with no family, occupation or personality, and so can be disposed of.

Why does such evil occur, and why are there no monsters involved, only ordinary people? Hannah Arendt also spoke of the lack of language among the perpetrators of such evil; if one is unable to apply words of all-pervasive custom to one's actions, such as "no murder', one cannot form the pervasive custom in one's brain.

Introduction by Christian Angerer and Franz Richard Reiter

From 1943 to 1945 Kambanellis was imprisoned in Mauthausen concentration camp, and later he wrote a book and poetry about his time there. Subsequently Mikis Theodorakis put four of his poems to music in the *'Mauthausen Cantata'*.

Mauthausen was liberated in May 1945. *'Mauthausen'*, written by long-term inmate Hans Marschalek and much admired by Kambanellis, first appeared in Greece in 1965 and was reprinted 40 times. These excerpts from Iakovos Kambanellis' subsequent publication *'Freedom Came in May'* were translated into English by Patricia Hughes B.A. Hons German, M.A. Politics.

This book begins with a short biography of Kambanellis. The excerpts from *"Freedom Came In May"* were produced and translated into German by Christian Angerer and Nina Aichberger and edited by Franz Richard Reiter. They tell of his experiences as a prisoner in Mauthausen and describe the concentration camp [i], its environment, and what occurred following liberation.

All four poems in the *'Mauthausen Cantata'* are included. You are encouraged to read the book and hear, sing and accompany the music.

Mauthausen Concentration Camp Memorial / Education:
www.mauthausen-memorial.org
education@mauthausen-memorial.org
www.erinnern.at
 ephelant-verlag.at
www.huesbooks.com

Iakovos Kambanellis

Iakovos Kambanellis was born 2nd December 1921 on the Greek island of Naxos. He was a child when his family moved to Athens as economic migrants. There he attended technical school and learnt graphic design. Insatiable for knowledge, he explored antique and bookshops, intrigued by philosophy, ancient theatre and international literature.

In October 1940 during the Second World War, fascist Italy led by dictator Benito Mussolini attacked Greece. Italian troops suffered many defeats, but Greece was defeated on 23rd April 1941 after a peripheral attack by the allied German Army on 6th April 1941 that led to invasion. The occupation was terrifying, with extreme hunger, despotism and mass shootings.

Kambanellis was 22 in 1942, when a friend persuaded him to flee to Switzerland. They took the train to Vienna, obtained forged Italian passports and continuing the journey to Innsbruck. Shortly before arrival, inspectors boarded the train and found Kambanellis' sketches; as a graphic designer he had made sketches of his feelings and opinions and carried them with him. Combined with his forged Italian passport, they guaranteed his arrest for political dissension.

He was initially taken to Elisabeth Promenade prison in Vienna, then to a containment camp, then finally on 15th October 1943 to Mauthausen concentration camp, where he remained in custody until liberated by the allies on 5th May 1945.

Despite being no underground fighter, Kambanellis' confinement in the concentration camp made him join the resistance. 150 Greek women whom the Americans had forbidden to go to Palestine after liberation begged him not to abandon them, not to disappear. For that reason he remained in the camp longer than expected, and only left alongside his 'protégées'. Later he became a political representative for the government.

After his return Kambanellis found himself drawn to theatre and film. However his ambition to be an actor was not attainable, although it didn't take him long to be recognised for scriptwriting and drama; nowadays he is viewed as the 'father' of modern Greek theatre. His Mauthausen book is still his only piece of prose. He wrote poems only when he could use them in plays. All of his scriptwriting skills were used almost exclusively for film and theatre. After his death, an Athens theatre company put his much-read book about Mauthausen onto the stage.

The 'Mauthausen Cantata' shows how the Greeks lived in the concentration camp. The presentation of the book begins with Theodorakis' music sung by virtuoso Maria Farantouri, who has continued to perform the 'Mauthausen Cantata' since it first appeared. She visits Kambanellis' daughter as she deals with her parents' personal effects, and speaks with actors and a very well-known Greek director who put many of Kambanellis' works on stage. Manolis Glezos talks of the childhood and youth he shared with Iakovos Kambanellis on the island of Naxos, where nowadays a small theatre museum reminds visitors of the author's life and times. Meanwhile in Athens an actor and an actress perform a key scene from 'Mauthausen' in front of the camera.

Kambanellis eventually became Greece's most important 20th century playwright. He died in Athens aged eighty-nine on 29th March 2011.

'Freedom Came in May'

On the 5th May 1945 the first American tank rolled through the gates of Mauthausen. This book begins with liberation of the concentration camp and the months following, when thousands of inmates had no choice but to remain there. Iakovos details his memories of the camp, how locals behaved while it existed, and reactions to the liberation in the locality.

As a prisoner he describes the routine inmate's day of hunger, cold, illness and the volatility of the SS. He tells of individual acts of resistance, and relates the mass escape of Soviet officers, most of whom were slaughtered by the SS or locals, who cynically referred to all escape attempts as "Mühl district hare-hunting".

After liberation Kambanellis fell in love with 19-year-old Jannina, a Lithuanian inmate. Ironically when her Italian husband arrived to take her home she was unable to relate to him after all she had been through.

Kambanellis describes not only personal experiences, but also various individual lives. He describes SS men holding sway over life or death to torture or murder inmates, even though at times they were defeated, for example by an intrepid, humanitarian Greek inmate called Andonis. Kambanellis reports that shortly before the end of the war SS soldiers began socializing with inmates, so that they would be acquitted more easily if called before the courts. He tells how inhabitants of local villages and farms seldom showed any sympathy for inmates, although a few did assist. "This is the truth as I remember it," Kambanellis wrote in the foreword to his book, "while spending hours looking at old notes and struggling to cast my mind back."

When Kambanellis returned to Athens many people probed him about what had really occurred in Mauthausen; a newspaper asked for an article. Kambanellis gave them hand-written notes about the "pain, shock, martyrdom, hope and paranoia in this camp" after liberation. It was published in 1965 as *Freedom Came In May* in 38 chapters.

Concentration Camp and Environment

Since daybreak we have been travelling in goods wagons. It's pitch black. Most of us have already had forty days of solitary confinement and spent four months in a small camp near Simmering.

There was a Jew there as well. The SS encircled him and screamed "Ball!" Then the Jew began to run from one to another and they kicked him in the legs, the stomach, the ribs, and the head. The football game ended when the 'ball" was lying motionless in blood and mire. After they got bored with playing the same game day after day, they drowned him in a river.

The train stopped at many stations, and the other carriages were quite normal; passengers got out of the same train and others got in. They were speaking low and putting their ears to the walls. We heard conversations such as;
Woman: *"Tell Helga not to worry about the umbrella."*
Man: *"Did I take the rest of the money off the counter? Oh yes, here it is!"*
Other man: *"Have you got any more luggage?"*
Another man: *"That's all, thank you."*
Another man: *"Stop sir! My name is Gandert ...*

Have a good journey!"
Another woman: *"Helmut, don't treat me as stupid..."*
Man: *"Rubbish, I'll be back by Tuesday."*

We hear all the tannoys and the stationmaster's whistle but we don't know where we are or where we're going. We stop again. This time they unbolt the sliding doors and open them. It's still daytime; the sun is shining directly into our faces and blinding us, but even so, it's much better.

The station is small, provincial, surrounded by trees and fenced off by the SS. The officer requests passengers getting out to move on quickly, and those ready to get in to wait a minute. The transfer to Mauthausen SS is done by name; we are put into rows of five. Passengers on the platform and in carriages hardly notice us; neither do railway workers. One of them, obviously inspector, is sat on the step with an open thermos drinking coffee.

All of this represents "good signs" to us. Hope springs eternal, helped by the afternoon sunshine and a giant smiling face winking at us from a beer advertisement. The nearest to me whispers, "It looks as if we're going to work in the village." Another says "In the fields at the worst." Then another one says "French prisoners do well, working in the fields. Lots of them escape."

We go through the main road in the village, houses to left and right. Glancing through windows we see furniture inside: "Good signs." A man is standing on an armchair wiping the window shutters, a woman leaning out of the window. Schoolgirls ride past on bikes; they stand still; we hear them calling something to the SS men, something about "the film at the cinema tonight". We're not allowed to speak to each other but we get the picture..." Good signs, good signs."

The path leads past shops. People are doing their shopping, and most of them greet the SS men. One man with razor foam on his face comes out of the hairdressers and calls out to the SS officer who's just underwritten the transfer, "Don't forget! My place at nine o'clock along with Anni! Agreed?"
"He's going to get married," we all think. "Anni's his wife-to-be. He could be having children. Good signs."

We come to a square. The Danube slinks wearily past on the left. There's a notice on a post: helmet on head, finger pressed to the mouth and below: "Learn to be silent, don't chatter."

We've hardly crossed the square when the officer cries, "Halt!" A ball of wool rolls between the feet of the group of five in front of me. The SS man lifts his foot and, with his boot heel, stamps over and over again on the toes of anyone who steps on the wool. Then he picks it up, goes to the bakery door as he rolls it up, and hands it to the woman standing there.

"Forward March!" Gradually the houses get further and further apart and we're marching on a broad, unsurfaced road between estates. The sun has gone down; it's fresh; cows now and then. It's the beginning of the back of beyond. We can't see any more houses; can still hear cows. We see another notice on another post: "Do not trespass. Trespassers will be arrested and shot without warning."

A little further on a little wooden crucifix, like those believers put up at crossroads in Austria and Germany; roughly ten milk tins next to it. "Halt!" To right and left, sentry huts. In the middle, a boom barrier for vehicles: "Mauthausen Concentration Camp."

On both sides of the sentry huts there's a fence made of narrow rows of barbed wire up to three metres high leading away into the distance, losing itself in the woods and the night that's already fallen.

We have no more illusions. Mauthausen is seen like a fortress in the background on the crest of the hill, the path lit by a long row of electric light bulbs. The nearer we get, the clearer the details. High stone walls; barbed wire above electrical isolators; high stone towers with machine guns; signs of skull bandages on the gable points; a chimney spitting out fire - spitting out fire, just like oil refiners!

The air stinks of burnt flesh; we realise that the pebbles on the path are mixed up with charred remains and pieces of bone. Nobody murmurs. Who could dare to say, "Do you know they make soap and other chemical products from human beings?"

Everybody Knew

During National Socialism a rumour circulated that soap was being manufactured from prisoners murdered in the camps, which historical research could not prove. However the existence of the rumour reveals that everyone recognized the horrors of National Socialism. There is evidence that prisoners' gold teeth, hair and skin were recycled.

The Concentration Camp SS

We reach the path circumventing the SS barracks. To the right, the barracks with verandas and flowers. SS soldiers are sitting on jutting out bits of wall.

To the left there's a football field marked with white lines. Next to it there's a row of barracks fenced in with barbed wire and more electric isolators; the infirmary.

We walk up to the main gate, where the path is full of signs:

Post Office
Officers' Mess
SS Canteen
Dentist
Doctor
Work Units Management
Political Department
Commandant's Office

The gate opens. It has two wings, each one up to three meters high. To the left and right of each of them is a tower, and over the gate an SS man with a machine gun. As we pass the gate someone yells out, *"Work makes you free!"* [Arbeit macht frei!]

We try to translate it. Those who understand whisper to their neighbours: "'Work' means δουλειά, "'make' means κάνει, "'free' means ελεύθερος. "Making something makes you free." What on earth does that mean? Is it a German ritual? A bit of news? A promise?

The football field, the SS football team and spectators

"The last Austrian champion football team during the war was ATSV Mauthausen, often called Mauthausen I, or in contemporary reports SG (Sozialgemeinschaft or club) Mauthausen, made up of camp surveillance personnel."

Men who day after day tormented, hit and tortured prisoners would every Sunday afternoon put their football gear on to kick a ball against LASK, Urfahr FC, Hertha Wels, Welser FC, against forwards and amateurs of Steyr Kickers, against Linz Railways and Enns FC.

Up there in the concentration camp, the camp guards would play home games. The football field was on the south side of the camp, where they put a mass grave as soon as the war ended. Nowadays it's a meadow. Mauthausen people wanting to see the game were welcome as spectators.

Anton Weinzierl: *"Those days I was a boy, a trainee. I went up a few times to watch the games."*

Walter Kohl: *When the Mauthausen SS was Upper Austria's champion football team. Football in Nazi times, and the way it looked in newspapers.*
In: Michael John, Franz Steinmassl (publisher): *...when the grass burns ... 100 years of football in Upper Austria.* Grünbach 2008, pp. 83 – 85.

Reception of prisoners into the camp

We are standing inside. The gate closes behind us. The square is empty, brightly lit and nothing to see; a row of barracks on the left; stone buildings on the right.
The commandant is here with other officers. We hear that a corpse is missing; it should be 166 but it's 165. As he leaves, the commandant orders "The missing dead man is to be found!" The officers move off towards the square between the first building and the inside of the high wall. The 165 dead bodies are lined up on the cement, some on the stomach and others on the back. The counting starts again.
"What kind of corpses are these on the ground? Does anybody know?"
They order us to undress and bundle our clothes up. We have to put all of our belongings on a row of tables: clothes, watches, rings and gold, everything separate. From time to time the SS leader picks up a watch or a piece of jewellery from the personal effects and looks at it casually. If he likes it, he savagely punches the person it belongs to, screaming "Your gold watch, you dirty scumbag? You pig! I'll show you what that means, you filthy drudge!"
When all belongings are given up, inmates walk to the subterranean baths. We see the showers in

the low ceilings and we just wait.

Unexpectedly, other prisoners come in carrying razor blades and scissors and sit down on stools, with a pot of soapy water next to each one. We kneel in front of them and they cut and shave our hair, beards, under-arm hair, pubic hair. When shaving finishes they give a tiny piece of soap to each person and send us under the shower. We follow every movement to see what the barbers and the rest will do next. Are they going out? Are they leaving us here by ourselves? But they don't go.

Warm water flows all over us. Later on, we go back to the square, wet and shivering. They give us long pants, shirts, trousers, jackets and hats, all blue-and-white striped, and they also give us clogs.

A very tall prisoner, about 60 and bald with glasses, passes by and takes a good look at us. He's wearing ordinary clothes marked with red oil paint at the back and front, just like the rest of the old institutional prisoners in Mauthausen. He throws the cigarette he's smoking on the ground for one of us to craftily pick up, and asks the man doling out clothing "Where have this lot come from?"

As they lead us to the quarantine barracks we ask them, "Who were those 165 dead people?" They answer, "Just today's corpses."

Photo taken between 1942 and 1945 in the SS Mauthausen Identification Service. Taken from the "Photograph Archive of the Mauthausen Concentration Camp Memorial / Amicale Collection Paris". The identity of the man is unknown.

Excerpt 4. Taskmasters and forced labour in the camp

There are plenty of foreigners here too, like Russians, French and Czechs.
We find out we're staying two or three weeks in Mauthausen. After that they'll send us on, some to factories, some to outside detachments to reconstruct bombed bridges or rail tracks, others to the quarry. The ones that stay in central camp are much better off.
We also find out how the concentration camp functions and exactly what it is for. At the top is the Commandant or camp commander, the SS-Standard-bearer. He's called Ziereis and is friends with Himmler.
Under him comes the Vice Commandant, called Leader of Protective Custody, a very malicious man named Bachmayer, a lieutenant. All the others are the same rank: Schulz in the political department, and Altfuldisch, who decides who's working where. He is Upper Leader of Work Duties; Upper because the Forced Labour Office includes three officers below him, Spatzenegger, Trumm and Zoller, all lieutenants. Obviously there are lots more, but they are the main ones that handle us with no restraint. The SS officers are the leaders, with lower-ranking officers and soldiers in every office or job.
Even so their assistants and adjuncts are

confirmed, time-honoured prisoners. Many of them are convicts or famous criminals, brought here from different prisons to serve their time. They have green triangles on the chest that say "Take care when you see me!"

Others are political prisoners like teachers, academics and educated people, and they do all the office work. All the political prisoners have red triangles; Jews have yellow stars, gypsies and stateless people black triangles, and homosexuals pink ones.

Every barracks has a responsible person called the *block elder*, alongside a scribe and two chamberlains called the *room elders*, one set for every room.

Central camp prisoners work in the quarry, loading Danube sand into carriages and cars, building rooms for the camp and factory, and working in the fields. There's also plenty of other work; room attendants, joiners, smiths, decorators and painters, medical workers, cooks and corpse carriers. "But whatever you do, no matter where they send you or what you're assigned to do – make sure you never get ill; what cripples everybody is dysentery. Watch out, because as soon as they see you're ill they'll send you to the hospital, from where there's no escape. As soon as you get diarrhoea, you toast your bread on the coals and eat it like that. That's your only hope."

At half past eight it's silent, everyone in bed and lights out. In the morning at six we're all up and the beds are made. We grab half a litre of substitute coffee and go outside: it's forbidden to stay in the block. At seven we assemble in the main square to be counted. Our barracks contains 500 prisoners and we assemble in 10 rows of 50. The assembly square fills up with thousands of still, silent prisoners standing to attention. We are all counted and then the work detachments start to leave.

Pretty soon we know what a concentration camp is for; nobody needs to tell us. The work detachments in fenced-off areas of the camp return at midday for rations, while those on the outside, especially in the quarry, only return in the evening. With all this coming and going, thousands are being told once or twice a day as they go through the gate, "Work makes you free".

Newcomers believe this promise, and some are so blind that they see contradictory things all around and draw peculiar conclusions. It is better to hope. In any case, as long as the SS have no actual reason to wipe you out, obviously you'll go home alive one day; the opposite is illogical. But Elders deny this altogether and say, "Once you're in here, you don't get out." Certainly, Mauthausen 'work frees' you every time, but only if you think of death as freedom and the next life as your rightful home. The new ones are skeptical about such persistent pessimism and frustration. They think the Elders are trying to intimidate them, that somehow they profit from demoralizing them and creating profound despair. In fact the hopeless ones are fewer than the hopers; so it's better to stop listening to them, and continue hoping on, undisturbed, as much as you want to.

We who are not provisionally assigned to any work or detachments just obey bellowed commands from SS under-officers, and constantly chat to each other as we run around the assembly square in groups. The SS men are bawling that we are work-shy parasites; inexplicable to us. It all stops at the accursed noon assembly, never popular because counting us has been devolved to low ranking officers. To show their pride at replacing the higher ranks and to demonstrate what they are capable of, they pick out two or three prisoners and pummel them until they spew up blood; Jews and Russians are preferred. Horrific as it is, we are glad not to be them.

Before long we return to the barracks for rations; a litre of vegetable soup. There isn't enough cutlery, and spoons are in short supply; twenty people are eating with the same one, as it's forbidden to wash up before the food's doled out. The soup is some sort of white kohlrabi, as big as melons. Some are sick with the first mouthful, others with the last, others only taste it once. We are just at the start of it.

At six comes the evening roll call; the whole assembly square is full, just like it was this morning. Next we pick up the evening ration;

250 grammes bread, black as earth, and 20 grammes margarine. As soon as the rations are given out all kinds of barterers and black marketeers turn up from the other barracks to swap bread for two cigarettes, or margarine for half a one.

The whole time, flames are incessantly darting out of the oven chimney, day and night, and the air we breathe smells like burning flesh, human flesh.

Andonis

Kambanellis tells of Andonis, a Greek prisoner, on the 'life-ending steps', a long stone staircase in Mauthausen quarry where inmates had to heave heavy stone blocks up incessantly, dying in the process. Even today the monstrous long, steep staircase and shifting steps still make one shudder.

Andonis

Up there on the measureless steps,
On the high wailing spectrum,
In the steep 'Vienna grave',
In the quarry of woe,

Jews and thugs are swarming,
Jews and renegades are stumbling,
Heaving boulders on their backs,
Hauling stone for slaughter.

Andonis hears a voice nearby,
Gets wind of a man crying,
"Friend, oh, friend, oh comrade, mate,
Lend me a hand up these steps."

But far up there on the boundless steps,
On the steep ladder of anguish,

Assistance is contemptible,
Compassion is a curse.

The Jew collapses under the boulder;
His step becomes blood red.
"Oy! You, my lad, come over here
And fetch this twin-size hunk."

Me, I'll fetch three times as much.
That's me, I am Andonis,
And you, if you're a man, be brave!
Approach the marble reaping-yard."

Solidarity in the Concentration Camp

It's my second week in the quarantine barracks, just after noon and drizzling. The very tall, bald man with glasses that I first saw in front of the baths walks past - and returns. Standing in the middle of us he demands, "Who is the Athens boy?"

Uneasy, I look around at the others – what do they want of me? Then I see the sign on his jacket: red triangle, D in the centre, number nine thousand something; he's a political prisoner, a German, been in the camp at least two or three years. I don't know what else to do but say, "That's me."

The German steps up and looks at me for a minute through his glasses – his mouth trembles – and starts talking: *"Retsina, fenta, Faliro, dalassa, ena wari gliko."* He goes quiet and then starts again: *"Kalimera, kalispera, efcharisto, poli, simera, avrio, kokinelli, chero poli, marintes"*, an endless stream of hopelessly pronounced Greek words that sounds like music to my ears.

He breaks into wild, staccato laughter, goes quiet

again, takes out a big black cloth, and wiping the rain off his cheeks and bald head he says in German, word for word, *"I lived in Athens for three wonderful years, and every night we went to Faliro. I was business manager of a German Electro firm; I've got lots of Greek friends, good friends."*

He makes a note of my number on a pad: *"Three, seven, seven, three, four,"* then stuffs a packet of cigarettes into my pocket and shakes my hand. *"My name is Schneider, Wilhelm Johann Schneider... See you 'round!"* ... and he's off.

Two days later the barracks scribe asks me what a "graphic designer" like me does, and I explain that I studied at technical school and got a certificate. Being Czech he used his own language to say something like *"We'll do it hush-hush as you've got a diploma."*

He asked if I could write Latin script and whether I had nice handwriting; I said yes. He took me on as his assistant and handed me the personnel files to fill in using my own judgement.

"Write as slowly as you can, but not so that it looks as if you're doing it on purpose, so that I can keep you here until they've closed all access to factories and other dangerous places. Then we'll see what happens. And make sure you learn German as fast as possible. If an SS man speaks

to you in German and you answer, "Me no understand" I wouldn't want to be in your shoes. French is OK for us, but not for everybody. Compri? And one more thing: Not a word of this to anyone or you're lost – and we are too!"

Fritz Kleinmann (1923-2009) was imprisoned in Buchenwald, Auschwitz and Mauthausen camps during his youth.

Q: When you were in the concentration camps what gave you the strength to carry on? What kept you going?

A: "A legion of inmates looked after me again and again; that was very, very important to me. They protected, pulled strings and shielded me as far as they could, because I was a boy, but such incredible comradeship didn't guarantee anything. It's pure coincidence that I'm one of the twenty-six that survived the transport. To put it bluntly, I've slid off death's shovel a few times. There were phases – I'll tell you straight – when I was going to commit suicide. But I was lucky that my father was nearby. He was my source of strength. Once we had to stand outside the whole night in minus temperatures – we didn't know the exact temperature, of course – and he winked at me and said, "Move yourself lad, you're freezing," so I said, "Dad, how long can we carry on doing this?" he said, "Move yourself lad, we've gone through plenty of other things. We've got to get through this."[ii]

Life after Liberation

Suddenly Jannina and I could go for a 'totally free' walk on the Mauthausen road; but it was a long way uphill and Jannina became very tired.

To add to that, her military trousers were rough and coarse and they scraped her skin. For a moment she withdrew to pull her trouser bottoms further down. I ripped my handkerchief in two and bandaged her knees, seeing the skin on her ankles grazed and raw. When she pulled her trouser legs up over her knees she said that since the 5th of May she'd already gained four kilos. Meanwhile we'd given up on 'Sie'; I didn't call her 'Miss' and she didn't call me 'Mr'.[iii]

We sat down on the kerb to hitch a ride from a passing car. She leaned her back on my chest to stop me feeling cold, and I opened my jacket to wrap her inside it; the pair of us fitted inside easily; I put my arms around her as well. She soon felt comfortable and fell asleep, even snored a little. Her shaven head smelt of American soap.

From the bottom of the road a car headlight shone on the trees two or three times. *"Wake up,"* I insisted, *"there's a car coming,"* but she was deep asleep. The car was approaching fast. I just put her down carefully in the grass and stood up to signal the car to stop. Regrettably the minute I did my blood froze ...

The gang in the car were belting out a German ditty. "*Oh no, they're back,*" I whispered hoarsely. The Americans had suggested we watch out for "unsanitized SS nests" still in existence. Now the headlight was already on me.

In her sleep Jannina picked up the poisonous tune as well and became hysterical - screaming and stumbling around, bumping into trees, not knowing which way to turn ... I ran and grabbed her and hid her face in my jacket so they couldn't hear her cries. The car stopped; the ditty ended ...

Three soldiers with machine guns sprang out of the car and, in American, one shouted "Anybody there?"
All at once I could breathe again. "Yes," I said, "You are Americans, aren't you?"
"Do you need help?" the American asked and turned a big lamp on us.

We climbed into the car bursting with soldiers. They thought Jannina was a man; making a space on the bench, they said, "Sit here lad."
"Did you get lost?" the one with the lamp asked.
"We were scared stiff," I answered.
I wanted to scream, "Was that your kind of joke?" but the car just drove on with the soldiers

still roaring out 'their' German ditty as they did before:

> *Weighty, fruity smutty poo,*
> *Stinky, smelly doggy doo,*
> *Hallo, loo, loo,*
> *Loo, loo, loo ...*

They were all stamping on the bottom of the car, rolling eyes and bellowing wildly, exhilarated by triumph and imitating the SS. Jannina gained confidence and started to laugh, and a short time later she was singing with them. The same went for me: *"Freighted, fruited smutty poo..."*

They dropped Jannina at the women's barracks, with the soldiers saying "Good night young lady" to her this time.

When the War is Over

Lady with the frightened eyes,
Lady with the frozen hands,
Please don't lose sight of me
  When the war is over.

Travel on past the gate,
Jewel of the world!
Here's to kissing on the road,
Embracing in the square.

Lady with the frightened eyes,
Lady with the frozen hands,
Please don't lose sight of me
  When the war is over.

We'll make love in the stone quarry,
Down there the gas chambers,
Up inside the watchtowers,
And right up there on the steps.

Lady with the frightened eyes,
Lady with the frozen hands,
Please don't lose sight of me
  When the war is over.

Let's caress each other in daylight
Over the graves of corpses
Until their shadows grow dim.

Lady with the frightened eyes,
Lady with the frozen hands,
Please don't lose sight of me
When the war is over.

The concentration camp location and the local community

I found a note from Schneider stuck on my pillow. "As soon as you are back come and see me at the prison. We'll drink some whisky where they died for two drops of water."

The committee and the Americans had transferred direction of the prisons to Schneider. I just showed my pass to the soldiers and told them "Dr Schneider" had requested my presence.

It was the first time I'd been there. I looked at the row of locked doors, so quiet! Impossible to believe that behind every door there was an SS man, like Toller, Trumm or Fassel, under custody! Impossible that there was any space left in cells nowadays... and such a petrifying silence!

Schneider was sat in the prison office, surrounded by all kinds of photos, notes and documents.

"Sit down. Have you ever had a go at drinking this? Well, you can see what it is – whisky. They're all idiots, the Germans! A madman yells out 'We don't want butter, we want canons!' and they believed him! English or Americans wouldn't ever trust anybody saying 'We don't want whisky, we want canons!' That's why Germans are always losing the war. Whenever they can, they stop believing in butter and start trusting canons... No problem if you don't like the whisky, everything is difficult until you understand it... "

"Colonel Seibel requested me to take over the prisons and also to assist the American military court in writing Depositions. I was on the brink of leaving the day after tomorrow, but for this kind of work it's a pleasure to stay. I'll be much happier going home if I'm sure that none of them are getting off the hook."

"I gave your name so that you can make a Deposition. Casimir Clementes, Matys, Ballina and Milan Slansky are making Depositions too. Here are the books you hid. The Americans said you deserve a medal... I've had a bed brought in too, so I don't waste time in the barracks. There's so much to do... "

"You can be sure I'll deal with every single one of these murderers justly, just like Nietzsche und Rosenberg. Until I'm a hundred per cent sure that enough files exist to sentence them all to 'death by hanging' there's no point in leaving Mauthausen.

'What are they doing now?" I ask Schneider.

"How are they getting on?"

"They're not saying anything. They are contemplating. Ha, ha! There you are, they've just begun to think! Suddenly they've discovered their brains! But don't be fooled, if they took up the same posts again they'd do just the same or worse! But this lot here is going to be sentenced and hanged. Just as well!"

"But what about the other ones, who's going to judge them? Millions and millions of citizens knew everything and looked the other way – who's going to pass sentence on them? You think all these murders happened in secret – in Auschwitz, Dachau, Gusen and Mauthausen? Stupid! It all began with the fêtes and the singing in Munich and Berlin in 1933! If anybody told me he didn't have any idea what was going on I'd bash his head in. Do you think all these supposedly sweet-tempered farmers up to 50 kilometers around here didn't know what was going on in the camp? Is it credible that they never grasped it in all the six years that the camp existed? Maybe they never saw the work detachments - prisoners thin as skeletons - , all over the village, on the building sites, or on the railway platforms?"

"Every one of them knew about it. The whole of Germany did, from one end to another, and I'm going to prove it. I've got provisional evidence ready here in my pocket, so if anybody objects – the so-called ignorant German citizens – I can break every bone in their bodies."

"Take a good look at this map of Germany before it goes to the devil! Can you see all these circles? I've marked all the concentration camps. Every circle has a 50-kilometre radius. So what does that mean? Half of Germany is within the circles. So half of Germany knew about concentration and extermination camps! In consequence, dear boy, it is hard to believe that half the Germans knew about it and the other half were ignorant. Anyway, in captured territories the Army brought about the same bestialities as the SS in the camps, just as easily. Everybody knew! They all knew! Don't believe a word they say! Don't believe anybody! If they're lying to themselves it means they don't want to back down."

Schneider had been ranting and he walloped the table with his fist. Then he collapsed into an armchair and buried his face in his hands.
"Have a bit of whisky."
"Go to sleep. Go to sleep. I'll be a lot better tomorrow, in the morning."

A week before that sort of outburst from Schneider would have surprised me, but not any more. Casimir Clementes told me something I didn't know about before. The Gestapo shot Schneider's sister and her Jewish husband while they were attempting to flee. They had been helping his father, who was deported to Dachau and died there. That was the reason they arrested Wilhelm and brought him into Mauthausen.

I went back to my barracks, sat on my bed and looked out at the barbed wire on the fence. Once upon a time the dark wire was electrified; in contrast now they were well lit, so that nobody got accidentally hurt by touching them.

I was depressed, irritable. We had been so traumatized, Jannina and I, hearing that German song on the road... and then the prisons with the SS officers inside, and everything that Schneider had ranted about... everything was going round and round in my head. I lay down to sleep and just like every other night I began turbulently tossing and turning, over and over– and I couldn't suppress this despotic image:

"Imagine you are waking up to the piping out of reveille... You see SS men slowly walking past the rows and counting... and you realize that the arrival of the Americans was only a dream... Is this the first time you've dreamed that? Carry on with your bewitching delusion as long as you can, you idiot! Why are you trying to rest, to sleep? Get out of bed, get your clothes on and go for a walk!"

No State within A State

Each concentration camp was not an isolated state within a state. Practically all the local councils, loads of local businesses and heaps of local entrepreneurs were working with Mauthausen. Nutrition Office officials rationed the available food; judges and registrars recorded deaths; councillors granted building permission; health officials registered 'epidemics'; and military service stations supervised conscripts, all within the camps. Employment offices assigned the prisoners to factories producing lots of goods used by the entire camp, from barracks to crematorium. Engineers installed electricity and plumbing in the camps. Prisoners who fled were hunted, not only by the SS and the police, but also by Hitler Youth, the Land Army and the Foresters. SS officers lived in all the local villages where they visited pubs and cinemas, got engaged or married, or just went for a walk in uniform.[iv]

Notes

[i] 1938-45

[ii] Excerpt from a conversation with Fritz Kleinmann in 'We have to talk about this; Students Question Concentration Camp Inmates' published by Monika Horsky. Vienna 2015-2016, pp.69-70.

[iii] They were talking to each other informally because they felt close to each other.

[iv] http://www.doew.at/Service/Ausstellungen/1938.NS-Terror in Österreich/Das KZ Mauthausen/Umfeld – Aufbau des Lagers

www.ingramcontent.com/pod-product-compliance
Lightning Source LLC
Chambersburg PA
CBHW021329190426
43193CB00040B/887